FINANCIAL
FOOTPRINT VENTURES

Standard Deviation

&

The Stock Market

When I was in school, I was not exposed to any aspect of financial literacy. Bank accounts, retirement accounts, annuities, or even how to balance a checkbook were not covered in any mathematic or economic course I completed. This project was developed as a way to learn about investing while you actually invest! Warren Buffet & Benjamin Graham became billionaires and many others have become millionaires off of investing in the stock market. Yes, people have lost tremendous amounts of money in the stock market also; but within this project you will learn valuable investment lessons, and lose at most $5 (if you participate in the competition). You will hopefully select profitable companies by using the same investment ratios the professional's use. Then, you will track and chart the volatility of your companies' stock prices by using standard deviation. All of this may sound really confusing now, but once you begin to explore these concepts, they will all make sense. All of the documentation within this text will walk you through what I stated above. If you remain open minded to this text you will develop stock investing skills. With those skills you will have the confidence to open up a stock brokerage account and start making your own money off of stocks!

First Printing: 2018; Reprint 2025

ISBN: 978-0-9969033-3-2

Email: greg@gplpublishing.com
Website: gplpublishing.com
http://www.lulu.com/spotlight/gplpublishing.com

As you acquire this text **Standard Deviation and the Stock Market (Learner Workbook)** make sure you pick up the accompanying text,

Standard Deviation and the Stock Market: Instructors Guide
ISBN: 978-0-9969033-4-9

Ordering Information:

Special discounts are available on quantity purchases by corporations, associations, educators, and others. For details, contact the publisher at the above listed address.

FINANCIAL
FOOTPRINT VENTURES

Significance of the QR Codes

Link: l.ead.me/bgAFjG

Throughout this entire document you will see QR codes like the one above. Each QR code unlocks videos and resources for that individual section. You will be able to research and practice concepts right at the moment of confusion. With technology opening doors to new ways in which we obtain information, having immediate access to content in real time makes the content more relatable and easier to digest

Table of Contents

QR Code = **QR**

Create "Interest" Activities

Selecting Stocks

FINANCIAL
FOOTPRINT VENTURES

Narrowing down Stock Selection by using Accounting Ratios

1st Industry

2nd Industry

Using Standard Deviation to Measure Risk

Stock Market Simulation, Tracking Volatility, Current Research of Companies

FINANCIAL
FOOTPRINT VENTURES

Mathematics Standards Covered

Investing Websites – Start generating Passing Income Now!

Scope and Sequence/Unit Calendar

Contact Information

My Email: greg@gplpublishing.com
(Please email me regarding any questions you have about the project.)

"Invest in the Stock Market Main Page"
https://investinthestockmarketfpv.blogspot.com/
This option leads you to the Standard Deviation and the Stock Market link below, Stock market game websites, links for when the Stock Market Competition Begins, and the list of past winners when this text was taught in my classrooms. With just a $5 investment, you can see the type of winnings students received (for those that invested).

"Standard Deviation and the Stock Market Resources"
https://standarddeviationstockmarketlinks.blogspot.com
This option leads you to the resources you will need to research stock selection and the basics of standard deviation. All pages are lined up with the links perfectly. If something is confusing or does not show, email me so I can make quick changes to the site.

"Once the Stock Market Competition Begins"
https://oncethestockmarketcompetitionbegins.blogspot.com/
This option leads you to the resources you will need to stay up to date with your selection – post research! This site includes places to find current financial news, graphics/visual data on stocks, various financial calculators, websites and television shows with updated stock information and standard deviation documents and software.

FINANCIAL
FOOTPRINT VENTURES

To: All participants
From: Instructor

Hello! With this text you will dive in to the world of investing, specifically stocks. We are going to choose stocks based on met financial criteria, develop methods for picking or selling stocks, understand the link between past performance and future predictions and many other aspects of investing in the stock market. The plan is to have monetary prizes for the top 3 teams that show the greatest return on investment at the end of the competition.

This is why I am asking all participants to invest $5 towards the money pot. This way, you, will have a direct view of the risk and rewards of investing. For the "investment" of $5, you have the opportunity to win up to $50 for each person (third place) or up to $80 each person (grand prize). These numbers are tabulated based upon estimations of all participants investing $5

I will provide a receipt upon payment (for those that may need it for tax purposes). The $5 investment should be provided to me as soon as possible; this will help me structure the prize winnings for the top 3 winning teams.

Thank you.

Please cut off and return with the $5 investment.

_____ Yes, this is an excellent idea and my child is participating. (If money is an issue than come and talk to me, we can work something out.)
_____No. If no, please provide reason.

_____

Participant Name_____

Parent Name_____

Para: Todos los participantes
De: El instructor

¡Hola! Con este texto te sumergirás en el mundo de la inversión, especialmente en la bolsa. Seleccionaremos acciones según criterios financieros, desarrollaremos métodos para seleccionar o vender acciones, comprenderemos la relación entre el rendimiento pasado y las predicciones futuras, y muchos otros aspectos de la inversión en bolsa. El plan es ofrecer premios monetarios a los 3 mejores equipos que muestren el mayor retorno de la inversión al final de la competición.

Por eso les pido a todos los participantes que inviertan $5 para el bote. Así, podrán ver directamente los riesgos y las recompensas de invertir. Por la "inversión" de $5, tendrán la oportunidad de ganar $50 cada uno (tercer lugar) hasta $80 cada uno (gran premio). Estas cifras se tabulan con base en estimaciones de todos los participantes que invierten $5.

Proporcionaré un recibo al realizar el pago (para quienes lo necesiten a efectos fiscales). La inversión de $5 debe serme entregada lo antes posible; esto me ayudará a estructurar los premios para los 3 equipos ganadores.

Gracias.

Por favor corte y devuelva con la inversión de $5.

_____ Sí, esta es una idea excelente y mi hijo/a va a participar. (Si el dinero es un problema, venga y hable conmigo, podemos llegar a un acuerdo.)
_____ No. Si la respuesta es no, por favor indique la razón.

_____

Nombre del participante _____

Nombre del Padre _____

FINANCIAL
FOOTPRINT VENTURES

This is the start of you turning $5 into a profit!

What is an investment?

_____

_____

_____

_____

_____

_____

Phrase of Caution

Keep in mind that putting money into an investment **does not always ensure profit** many have lost their entire bank accounts off of poor investments. The people that **do the necessary research before selecting a company** are the ones that usually turn a profit.

Investment Scenarios

1). Would loaning a friend $10 to buy a movie ticket be considered an investment? Defend your position below.

_____

_____

2). If a person invested $10,000 to start a small computer repair service but lost most of that money in the first three months, would this be considered an investment? Justify your answer below.

_____

_____

3). Imagine that you have made an investment by buying one of only 3 known autographs of Michael Jackson. Shortly afterward, you hear that an auction house has just announced the discovery of 100 pieces of clothing with his original signature on each piece. Predict what you think will happen to the value of your investment? Make sure you support your answer with clarifying statements.

_____

_____

4). If a company makes an excellent product that you enjoy using, would it be a wise decision to invest in that company's stock?

_____

_____

5). If your mother/father asked you to invest your Christmas money into this idea/product/company they heard of, what pertinent questions would you ask? Minimum of 3 questions.

_____

_____

_____

Personal Inquiry

Statistically speaking, people in inner-city areas invest much less than people in more affluent areas. Provide reasons as to why you think this is.

_____

_____

_____

FINANCIAL
FOOTPRINT VENTURES

Financial instruments (**stocks**, bonds, mutual funds) are excellent sources of investments for the following 2 reasons:

1). They are considered **Liquid Assets.** This means they can be easily sold when the investor is ready to sell. Tangible items can take a while to sell.

2). Upon research the **rate of return** or **Profit** can be calculated before money is placed into the investment. Some companies pay investors **dividends (the income received from the sharing of a company's profit)** from them owning their stock. In this way, the investor has an idea of what to expect before the investment has even been made.

What does it mean to invest in stocks?

_____

_____

_____

Benefits/Drawbacks of Investing in Stocks

> *Phrase Bank:* Ownership and Voting Rights, Volatility and Risk, Requires Time and Knowledge, Easy to Invest, Tax Implications, Dividend Income, Competing Against Professionals, Potential for Higher Returns, Liquidity

Benefits	*Drawbacks*

FINANCIAL
FOOTPRINT VENTURES

Why is Picking a Stock like Preparing for a Relationship/Marriage?

My students were knee deep into this project when a student named "Julian" said the following: "Mr. Lakey, this sucks! My stocks are doing terribly, but we are not allowed to sell all of our shares in losing companies! Dumping my girlfriend is easier than dumping my stocks!" The class erupted in laughter, because they understood exactly what he was saying. Through my conversations and personal experience, I have generated 5 key ways in which selecting a stock is like preparing for a relationship/marriage. What do you think they might be?

1st way:_____

Reason why:_____

2nd way:_____

Reason why:_____

3rd way:_____

Reason why:_____

4th way:_____

Reason why:_____

5th way:_____

Reason why:_____

FINANCIAL
FOOTPRINT VENTURES

What is Dividend Income?

_____

_____

_____

Calculating Dividend Income Examples

Dividends Income = Number of owned Shares X Dividend Per Share

1). If you own 100 shares and the company pays a $0.68 dividend per share, what is your total Dividend Income?

> [ ]

2). You own 200 shares of Coca Cola (KO). The company pays a quarterly dividend of $0.46 per share. What is the annual dividend payout?

> [ ]

3). You hold 500 shares of a Real Estate Investment Trust (REIT) that pays a monthly dividend of $0.15 per share. What is the annual dividend payout?

> [ ]

4). Bill Gates: Owns 54,826,786 shares of Canadian National Railway Company (CNI). The company has paid out $2.38 per share over the last 12 months. What was his dividend income from this one stock?

> [ ]

Selecting Stocks based on Interest

There are 2 ways I have selected stocks. I). Use tips and accounting ratios (which will be used throughout this text), Or II). Selecting stocks based upon "interest". On pages 17 and 18, I have images of how I used interest boxes with my own children. **Remember –** this method below does not utilize any financial numbers of the company, just a simple way to tap into student interest.

Directions

In each of the four boxes below state a different interest/industry (animals, electronics, food, etc..) that you really enjoy – Diversification!

Once you have identified an interest/industry, find 1 to 2 publicly traded companies within that interest/industry; select company names you are familiar with, have affordable share prices, or both.

When all boxes are filled in, select the company names and/or share prices that work best for you.

Interest/industry_____ 1st Company _____ Ticker_____Share Price_____ 2nd Company_____ Ticker_____Share Price_____	Interest/industry_____ 1st Company_____ Ticker_____Share Price_____ 2nd Company_____ Ticker_____Share Price_____
Interest/industry_____ 1st Company_____ Ticker_____Share Price_____ 2nd Company_____ Ticker_____Share Price_____	Interest/industry_____ 1st Company_____ Ticker_____Share Price_____ 2nd Company_____ Ticker_____Share Price_____

Selecting Stocks based on Interest - Image

My daughter Bryce (8 years old) (10-13-20)

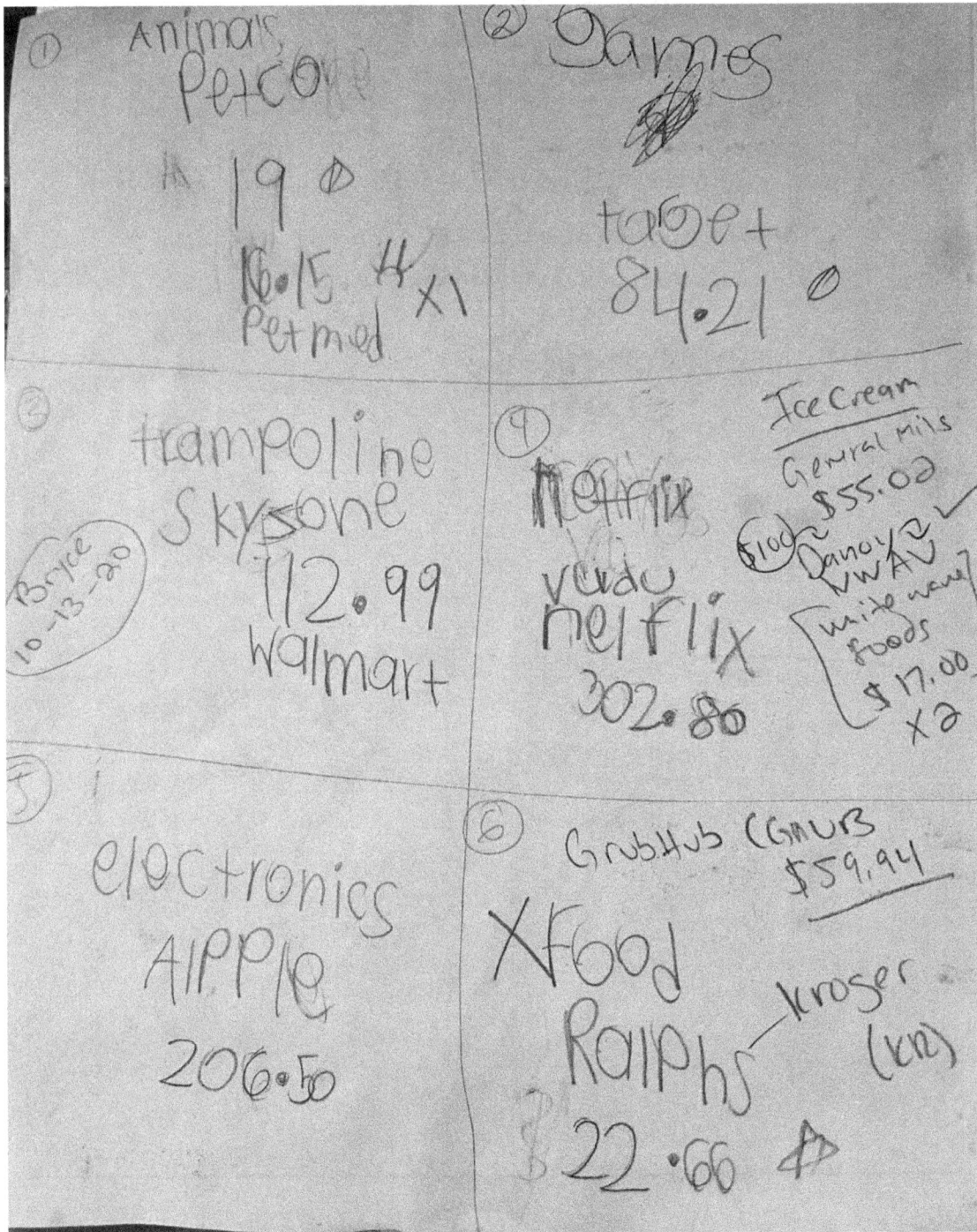

Selecting Stocks based on Interest - Image

My son Haidyn (11 years old) (10-13-20)

FINANCIAL
FOOTPRINT VENTURES

10 tips for picking winning stocks

Link: l.ead.me/bgAGdn

- Label the tip
- Provide an explanation of the tip

1) _____

2) _____

3) _____

4) _____

5) _____

6) _____

7) _____

8) _____

9) _____

10) _____

Reading Stock Data

On the link "Interpreting Stock Data"
Fill in the answers below to the best of your ability.

Link: l.ead.me/bgAGdn

1A) 52 week High

_____

1B) 52 week Low

_____

2) Company Name and Type of Stock

_____

3) Ticker Symbol

_____

4) Dividend Per Share

_____

5) Dividend Yield

_____

6) Trading Volume

_____

7A) Day High

_____

7B) Day Low

_____

8) Close

_____

9) Net Change

_____

FINANCIAL
FOOTPRINT VENTURES

Additional Vocabulary to Define

10) Bear Market

_____

11) Bull Market

_____

12) Initial Public Offering (I.P.O)

_____

13) Crowd Funding

_____

14) Institutional Investing

_____

15) Commission

_____

16) Assets

_____

17) Liabilities

_____

18) Day Trader

_____

19) Mutual Fund

_____

FINANCIAL
FOOTPRINT VENTURES

Contextual Example

If it is difficult to think of companies that are not household names (Meta, SpaceX, Apple), you can conduct research from the lens of "enhancing" something around you. For this mathematics section (Standard Deviation through the Stock Market) you will dive into the world of stock market investing. You and your group members will become **"institutional investors"** (a group of people) that will invest $1,000,000 in a **mutual fund** (a collection of stocks from different industries you combine together). The group with the highest rate of return will win the competition. You will also explore the world of **"Day Trading"** which is making stock transactions within the same trading day before the market closes. You are going to research and invest in companies that provide specific money-making characteristics. To do so, you must think about what "Industries" are going to impact you the most and what companies are intriguing within those industries.

Link: l.ead.me/bgAGdn

Different types of Industries

Water Utilities	Gas Utilities	Food
Cleaning Products	Computers (Wholesale)	Entertainment
Networking and Communication Devices	Education and Training Services	Internet Service Providers
Scientific and Technical Instruments	Banking	Personal Computers
Waste Management	Construction	Application Software
Gaming Activities	Appliances	Electric Utilities
Sporting Goods	Solar	Credit Services

FINANCIAL
FOOTPRINT VENTURES

The following is an **EXAMPLE** of how you can categorize your industries and companies.

Industry	Brief Description of why you have chosen this industry	2 Companies to invest in	Market Capitalization Category
1st Industry Banking	This industry moves the money of the world.	Bank of America Citi bank	Ultra Cap Large Cap
2nd Industry Application Software	This industry is imperative for all technology usage.	Microsoft Oracle	Ultra Cap Ultra Cap

Market Capitalization Category is on page 25. Make sure you read that page, it is very important!

Follow the links below to locate other industries that are not listed on page 22.
- https://standarddeviationstockmarketlinks.blogspot.com
- https://oncethestockmarketcompetitionbegins.blogspot.com/
- Scroll down to "Websites to locate Industries/Companies"

On the next page you will pick 2 separate industries you feel bring you profit. Within each industry you will select 2 companies to analyze. The entire point of the following activity is to find 2 companies to begin analyzing by their financial numbers. The financial numbers will inform you of what company is a better decision. You make money when you pick the right company.

Industry	Brief Description of why you have chosen this industry	2 Companies to invest in	Market Cap Category
1st Industry			
2nd Industry			

__Market Capitalization Category__ is on the next page. Make sure you read that page, before you complete this one!

Link: l.ead.me/bgAGdn

FINANCIAL
FOOTPRINT VENTURES

Market Capitalization (Cap) Categories
(Amount of risk based upon the size of the company)

Market Capitalization Value – What is it?

The market cap is the most basic way to look at a company's market value (the perception of how *risky* the stock is) because it takes into account the **size** of the company.

Market Cap = Share Price X Number of Shares Outstanding

Stock Categories for Market Capitalization (Market Cap) Categories

Micro Cap (Under $250 million): These stocks are the smallest and the riskiest (the most volatile) available. Huge potential for tremendous growth or tremendous failure.

Small Cap ($250 million to $1 billion): These stocks fare better than the microcaps and still have plenty of growth potential. The key word is potential.

Mid Cap ($1 billion to $10 billion): For many investors, this category offers a good compromise between small caps and large caps. These stocks have some of the safety of large caps while retaining some of the growth potential of small caps.

Large Cap ($10 billion to $50 billion): This category is usually best reserved for conservative stock investors who want steady appreciation with greater safety. Stocks in this category are frequently referred to as Blue Chips.

Ultra Cap (Over $50 billion): These are the most consistent stocks; meaning these stocks are not as risky (volatile) as the other categories. But, they will not grow by much either. These stocks are frequently referred to as Mega Caps.

Remember – The smaller the cap, riskier the investment; the more potential for growth. The bigger the cap, the safer the investment; consistent, but not as much room for growth. What type of an investor are you?

Tip – The site for the stock market competition we are going to use mainly accepts domestic (United States) and not Foreign (International) stock exchanges. So, stocks that have a period (.) or a colon (;) in the ticker symbol is a foreign stock and may not be available. _If it looks really good then just keep it off to the side, when we start purchasing shares of our companies you can try to use it and see what happens._

Major Tip – Every year, the majority of students will just pick companies they have heard of when we start buying shares. **_You win this competition by picking companies that no one has heard of. Do you research and try to find a hidden gem!_**

Link: l.ead.me/bgAMry

Price to Earnings Ratio (P/E Ratio)

The price-to-earnings ratio is very important in analyzing a potential stock investment. It provides a measuring stick for comparing whether a stock is overvalued or undervalued. **Simply put, the p/e ratio is the price an investor is paying for every $1 dollar of company earnings. Earnings are the profit the company generates.**

The _P_ in P/E stands for the stock's _current price._ The _E_ is for _earnings per share._
P/E Ratio = Current Price / (EPS) Earnings Per Share

Example – A stock's current price is $24 and the earnings per share is $3. The P/E ratio is 24/3 or 8. This means you are paying $8 for the company to have $1 profit.

High P/E can mean
- Could be valued higher than what it is actually worth "or"
- Industry has high hopes for the corporation

Low P/E can mean
- The market has "no confidence" in the company "or"
- The market may have overlooked this corporation (could be a HIDDEN GEM)

FINANCIAL
FOOTPRINT VENTURES

1st Industry Name_____

Price to Earnings Ratio (P/E)

Here is the link you can go to for more information on this ratio.

To find the data you need, you must do the following:
- Click on the company's ticker symbol **(Go to "Yahoo finance" and type it in)**
- Once that is done a quick snapshot of the company will pop up.
- The information you need should be on the "Statistics" page, if not – then perform a different google search.

P/E Ratio of your 1st industry_____ (This is a great comparison point for your company.)

1st Industry 1st Company Name_____Ticker Symbol_____

Market Cap_____Market Cap Category_____

P/E Ratio_____

1st Industry 2nd Company Name_____Ticker Symbol_____

Market Cap_____Market Cap Category_____

P/E Ratio_____

Which company do you feel has the better P/E Ratio_____?

TIP: As you move throughout these ratios, check out the (1M), (6M), (2Y) etc... graphs. Those visuals can help you see the trends of the company.

Link: l.ead.me/bgAMry

Price to Book Ratio (PBR)

This measurement looks at the value the "market" places on the "book value" of the company.

Market (Cap) Value is dictated by what people think **(their perception of the stock)** based on the supply and demand of the stock market.

Book Value is the "Accounting Value" derived from their balance sheet (Also called "Net Worth" or "Stock Holder's Equity"). **What a company is actually worth.**

Market Value ÷ Book Value = Price to Book Ratio

This ratio is used to see if your company is actually worth **(book value)** *to what people* **think** *it is worth* **(market value).**

If the (PBR) is high the stock may be (**overvalued**) (BE AWARE).

The smaller the (PBR) the closer the market value is to the book value (This is what you are looking for).

Bonus: If your (PBR) is a decimal that is sweet! This means your book value (actual value) is greater than its market value (the market's perception). You may have found a great stock! Pick it so you can ride the wave when its market value begins to increase.

Link: l.ead.me/bgAN67

FINANCIAL
FOOTPRINT VENTURES

1ˢᵗ Industry Name_____

Price to Book (PBR) Ratio

To find the data you need, you must do the following:
- Click on the company's ticker symbol **(Go to "Yahoo finance" and type it in)**
- Once that is done a quick snapshot of the company will pop up.
- The information you need should be on the "Statistics" page, if not – then perform a different google search.

PBR of your 1ˢᵗ industry_____ (This is a great comparison point for your company.)

1st Industry 1ˢᵗ Company Name_____Ticker Symbol_____

Market Cap_____Market Cap Category_____

Price to Book Ratio_____

1st Industry 2ⁿᵈ Company Name_____Ticker Symbol_____

Market Cap_____Market Cap Category_____

Price to Book Ratio_____

Which company do you feel has the better Price to Book Ratio_____?

*(Meaning – What company is **actually (Book value)** performing close to its projections (Market Value)).*

Link: l.ead.me/bgAN67

Current Ratio

This ratio measures a company's ability to pay short-term obligations. To calculate the ratio, you need to compare current assets to current liabilities.

Current Assets = cash, accounts receivable, inventory and other assets that are expected to be turned into cash in less than a year.

Current Liabilities = accounts, wages, taxes payable, and the current portion of long-term debt

Current Ratio = Current Assets/Current Liabilities

A company with a current ratio of **less than one** does not have the capital on hand to meet its short-term obligations if they were all due at once.

For example, Company A has $400,000 in current assets and $500,000 in current liabilities. Company A will have a current ratio of 0.8/1. This means company A has $.81 cents in current assets for every $1 in current liabilities. It does not have enough to cover its debts.

A company with a current ratio that is **greater than one** indicates the company should be able to remain solvent (pay its debts).

For example, Company B has $200,000 in current assets and $80,000 in current liabilities. Company B will have a current ratio of 2.5/1. This means company B has $2.5 in current assets to pay for every $1 in current liabilities. It has more than enough to cover its debts.

Link: l.ead.me/bgANo5

FINANCIAL
FOOTPRINT VENTURES

1st Industry Name_____

Current Ratio

To find the data you need, you must do the following:
- Click on the company's ticker symbol **(Go to "Yahoo finance" and type it in)**
- Once that is done a quick snapshot of the company will pop up.
- The information you need should be on the "Statistics" page, if not – then perform a different google search.

Current Ratio of your 1st industry_____ (This is a great comparison point for your company.)

1st Industry 1st Company Name_____Ticker Symbol_____

Current Assets _____Current Liabilities_____

Current Ratio_____

1st Industry 2nd Company Name_____Ticker Symbol_____

Current Assets_____Current Liabilities_____

Current Ratio_____

Which company do you feel has the better Current Ratio_____?

(Meaning, which company has enough current assets to cover its current liabilities?)

Link: l.ead.me/bgANo5

Solvency – How dependent is your company on debt

Debt-to-Equity Ratio (D/E)

This is a very simple ratio. The debt to net equity ratio answers the question, **"How much does the company need debt (borrowed money) to finance its operations?"** A **low debt to equity ratio** indicates lower risk because the company relies less on sources outside of the business to finance growth. It has the cash to pay its debts. A **high debt to equity ratio** means a company may be in financial distress and could have difficulty paying its debts.

A low debt to equity ratio makes outsiders feel more comfortable in doing business with the company; especially banks that may provide a loan. Less debt and more equity reduces the chances of bankruptcy.

Total Assets = All money/property they _possess_.
Total Liabilities = All money/property that is _owed_ to other businesses.
Stockholders Equity = Total Assets – Total Liabilities

Debt to Equity Ratio = Total Liabilities/Stockholders Equity

For example, a company has $100,000 in liabilities and $50,000 in stock-holders equity. The debt-to-equity ratio is $2/$1. _This means the company has $2 in debt for every $1 of equity (net worth). What the company **owes** is twice as much as it owns._

The **Debt-to-Equity Ratio** is relative to the industry. Technology based business that have a lot of research and development costs can have a ratio of 2 or more. Large manufacturing and stable publicly traded companies have ratios between 2 and 5. In banking and other financially based businesses, it is not uncommon to see a ratio of 10 or even 20, but that is unique to those industries.

Link: l.ead.me/bgANqq

FINANCIAL
FOOTPRINT VENTURES

1ˢᵗ Industry Name_____

Debt-to-Equity Ratio (D/E)

To find the data you need, you must do the following:
- Click on the company's ticker symbol **(Go to "Yahoo finance" and type it in)**
- Once that is done a quick snapshot of the company will pop up.
- The information you need should be on the "Statistics" page, if not – then perform a different google search.

Debt to Equity Ratio of your 1ˢᵗ industry_____ (This is a great comparison point for your company.)

1st Industry 1ˢᵗ Company Name_____Ticker Symbol_____

Market Cap_____Market Cap Category_____

Debt to Equity Ratio_____

1st Industry 2ⁿᵈ Company Name_____Ticker Symbol_____

Market Cap_____Market Cap Category_____

Debt to Equity Ratio_____

Which company do you feel has the better Debt to Equity Ratio_____?

(Meaning, for every dollar the company OWNS, which one OWES the least amount of money.)

Link: l.ead.me/bgANqq

1st Industry Name_____

Now take the information you have gathered from the previous pages and decide which company out of this Industry you will select (marry) for all of intersession. *__Once we start buying shares you are not able to select different companies. If you marry a Stinker, you will not have a good time. Do the proper research before you decide.__*

1st Industry Company with best P/E Ratio:_____

1st Industry Company with best PBR:_____

1st Industry Company with best Current Ratio:_____

1st Industry Company with best D/E Ratio:_____

From the 4 ratios above select the one company within this industry that will be your final selection. If it is a tie, you must compare the graphs, the market cap categories, anything you can to make the best decision possible. You will not be able to **Divorce** your choice!

The final selection

Company Name_____

Company Ticker Symbol_____

FINANCIAL
FOOTPRINT VENTURES

Tip – The site for the stock market competition we are going to use mainly accepts domestic (United States) and not Foreign (International) stock exchanges. So, stocks that have a period (.) or a colon (;) in the ticker symbol is a foreign stock and may not be available. _If it looks really good then just keep it off to the side, when we start purchasing shares of our companies you can try to use it and see what happens._

Major Tip – Every year, the majority of students will just pick companies they have heard of when we start buying shares. **You win this competition by picking companies that no one has heard of. Do you research and try to find a hidden gem!**

2nd Industry Name_____

Price to Earnings Ratio (P/E)

P/E Ratio of your 2nd industry_____ (This is a great comparison point for your company.)

2nd Industry 1st Company Name_____Ticker Symbol_____

Market Cap_____Market Cap Category_____

P/E Ratio_____

2nd Industry 2nd Company Name_____Ticker Symbol_____

Market Cap_____Market Cap Category_____•

P/E Ratio_____

Which company do you feel has the better P/E Ratio_____?

•

Link: l.ead.me/bgAMry

2nd Industry Name_____

Price to Book (PBR) Ratio

PBR of your 2nd industry_____ (This is a great comparison point for your company.)

2nd Industry 1st Company Name_____Ticker Symbol_____

Market Cap_____ Market Cap Category_____

Price to Book Ratio_____

2nd Industry 2nd Company Name_____Ticker Symbol_____

Market Cap_____Market Cap Category_____

Price to Book Ratio_____

Which company do you feel has the better Price to Book Ratio_____?

*(Meaning – What company is **actually (Book value)** performing close to its **projections (Market Value))**.*

Link: l.ead.me/bgAN67

FINANCIAL
FOOTPRINT VENTURES

2nd Industry Name_____

Current Ratio

Current Ratio of your 2nd industry_____ (This is a great comparison point for your company.)

2nd Industry 1st Company Name_____Ticker Symbol_____

Current Assets _____Current Liabilities_____

Current Ratio_____

2nd Industry 2nd Company Name_____Ticker Symbol_____

Current Assets_____Current Liabilities_____

Current Ratio_____

Which company do you feel has the better Current Ratio_____?

(Meaning, which company has enough current assets to cover its current liabilities?)

Link: l.ead.me/bgANo5

2nd Industry Name_____

Debt to Equity Ratio (D/E)

Debt to Equity Ratio of your 2nd industry_____ (This is a great comparison point for your company.)

2nd Industry 1st Company Name_____Ticker Symbol_____

Market Cap_____Market Cap Category_____

Debt to Equity Ratio_____

2nd Industry 2nd Company Name_____Ticker Symbol_____

Market Cap_____Market Cap Category_____

Debt to Equity Ratio_____

Which company do you feel has the better Debt to Equity Ratio_____?

(Meaning, for every dollar the company OWNS, which one OWES the least amount of money.)

Link: l.ead.me/bgANqq

FINANCIAL
FOOTPRINT VENTURES

2nd Industry Name_____

Now take the information you have gathered from the previous pages and decide which company out of this Industry you will select (marry) for all of intersession. _Once we start buying shares you are not able to select different companies. If you marry a Stinker, you will not have a good time. Do the proper research before you decide._

2nd Industry Company with best P/E Ratio:_____

2nd Industry Company with best PBR:_____

2nd Industry Company with best Current Ratio:_____

2nd Industry Company with best D/E Ratio:_____

From the 4 ratios above select the one company within this industry that will be your final selection. If it is a tie, you must compare the graphs, the market cap categories, anything you can to make the best decision possible. You will not be able to **Divorce** your choice over intersession!

The final selection

Company Name_____

Company Ticker Symbol_____

Mean and Median Stock Price Notes

Now you will take your two final companies and find the Mean and Median stock prices over the last 13 months. Before that is to be done you will go to my blog or any other resource and take notes/examples on how to find the mean/median and what it stands for.

Link: l.ead.me/bgANz1

Notes/Examples for Mean

Notes/Examples for Median

FINANCIAL
FOOTPRINT VENTURES

1st Industry Company Name_____

Mean and Median Stock Price

Now, you have to find the last 12 or 13 month stock prices of both companies you selected in order to find the Mean and Median

To find the data you need, you must do the following:
- Click on the company's ticker symbol **(Go to "Yahoo finance" and type it in)**
- Once that is done a quick snapshot of the company will pop up.
- The information you need should be on the "Historical Prices" page, if not – then perform a different google search.
- The date will already be set a year from today (change the last option in blue to "monthly" then click "apply".
- Write down the "close" of the first 12 or 13 "monthly" dates.

*1st Industry Company Name*_____*Company Ticker*_____

Last 13 months stock prices

1)_____ 2)_____ 3)_____ 4)_____ 5)_____ 6)_____

7)_____ 8)_____ 9)_____ 10_____ 11)_____ 12)_____

13)_____

Mean Stock Prices of the last 12 or 13 years
(Show all algebraic work below - round answer to the nearest **hundredth place**)

Median Stock Prices of the last 12 or 13 months
(Show all algebraic work below - round answer to the nearest **hundredth place**)

2nd Industry Company Name_____

Mean and Median Stock Price

Now, you have to find the last 12 or 13 month stock prices of both companies you selected in order to find the Mean and Median

To find the data you need, you must do the following:
- Click on the company's ticker symbol **(Go to "Yahoo finance" and type it in)**
- Once that is done a quick snapshot of the company will pop up.
- The information you need should be on the "Historical Prices" page, if not – then perform a different google search.
- The date will already be set a year from today (change the last option in blue to "monthly" then click "apply".
- Write down the "close" of the first 12 or 13 "monthly" dates.

*2nd Industry Company Name*_____*Company Ticker*_____

Last 13 stock prices

1)_____ 2)_____ 3)_____ 4)_____ 5)_____ 6)_____

7)_____ 8)_____ 9)_____ 10_____ 11)_____ 12)_____

13)_____

Mean Stock Prices of the last 12 or 13 months
(Show all algebraic work below - round answer to the nearest **hundredth place**)

Median Stock Prices of the last 12 or 13 months
(Show all algebraic work below - round answer to the nearest **hundredth place**)

FINANCIAL
FOOTPRINT VENTURES

Standard Deviation Notes

Below, take notes or print out and staple/paste the notes on standard deviation.

Try to get a decent understanding of what standard deviation means (this will further assist you when you start bullying/selling shares of your companies).

Once you have finished taking notes and have a basic understanding, turn to the next 2 pages and analyze your 2 companies' stock prices through Standard Deviation.

Link: l.ead.me/bgAO5m

Notes/Examples for Standard Deviation

L₁	
	1st Industry Company Name_____ **Day**_____ **Company Ticker**_____ **Date**_____
	Standard Deviation (S.ID.2/3) – Use Stock Prices from last 12 months **1-Var Stats** n (Population size) = ∑x (Sum of population size) = $\bar{x}$ /μ (Mean/Average) = σ (Sigma: Standard Deviation) =

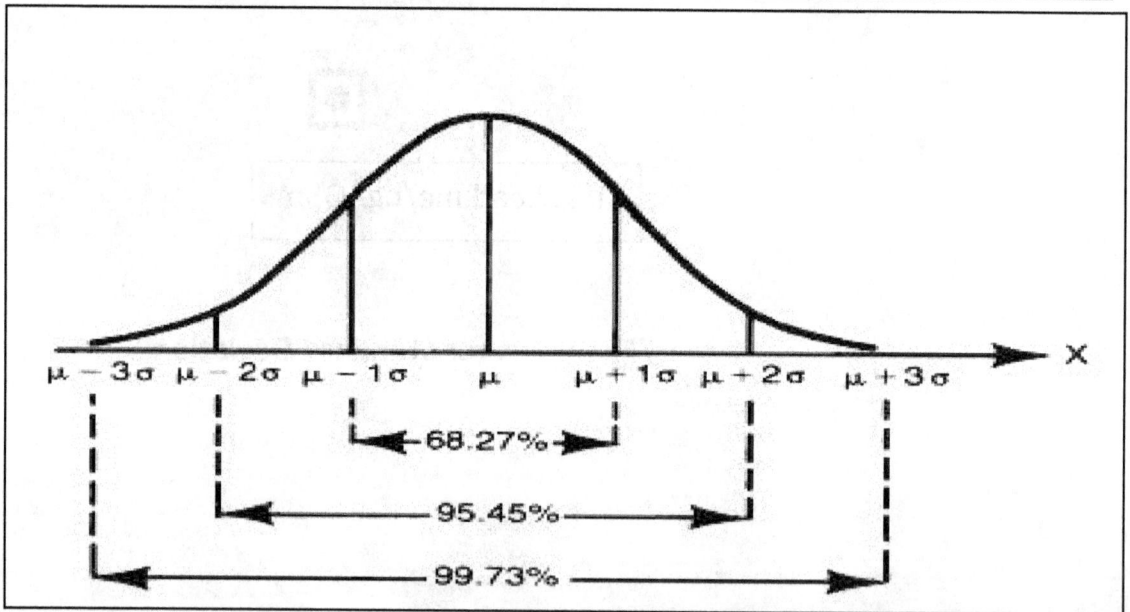

Based upon the data above, what does the standard deviation say about this particular stock's pattern of value at the 68%, 95% and 99% measure?

Looking at your "sigma" and your 99% measure, what is your view of this company's volatility (riskiness)?_____ Also, how will the volatility affect your decision to buy or sell shares of this company_____

L_1

2nd Industry Company Name_____ Day_____

Company Ticker_____ Date_____

Standard Deviation (S.ID.2/3) – Use Stock Prices from last 12 months

1-Var Stats

n (Population size) =

$\sum x$ (Sum of population size) =

$\bar{x}$ /μ (Mean/Average) =

σ (Sigma: Standard Deviation) =

Based upon the data above, what does the standard deviation say about this particular stock's pattern of value at the 68%, 95% and 99% measure?

Looking at your "sigma" and your 99% measure, what is your view of this company's volatility (riskiness)?_____ Also, how will the volatility affect your decision to buy or sell shares of this company_____

FINANCIAL
FOOTPRINT VENTURES

Group Investment Roles

Each student will be in charge of 2 stocks. Each student will write all 8 to 10 stocks below on their respective pages. When you have located the appropriate stocks (by **your** analysis) and have written them on this page you cannot change them! *__Make sure you place group members names next to the stocks they own!__*

Stocks You Will Invest In

Industry_____ Stock Name_____

Ticker_____Market Cap_____Market Cap Category_____

Industry_____ Stock Name_____

Ticker_____Market Cap_____Market Cap Category_____

Industry_____ Stock Name_____

Ticker_____Market Cap_____Market Cap Category_____

Industry_____ Stock Name_____

Ticker_____Market Cap_____Market Cap Category_____

Industry_____ Stock Name_____

Ticker_____Market Cap_____Market Cap Category_____

FINANCIAL
FOOTPRINT VENTURES

Industry_____ Stock Name_____

Ticker_____Market Cap_____Market Cap Category_____

Industry_____ Stock Name_____

Ticker_____Market Cap_____Market Cap Category_____

Industry_____ Stock Name_____

Ticker_____Market Cap_____Market Cap Category_____

Industry_____ Stock Name_____

Ticker_____Market Cap_____Market Cap Category_____

Industry_____ Stock Name_____

Ticker_____Market Cap_____Market Cap Category_____

Virtual Stock Market Game Options

http://www.smartstocks.com	**Basic Stock Game Rules I use**
http://www.virtual-stock-exchange.com	-$1,000,000 Per group -Minium $100 invested in each company (cannot be less than $100)
https://www.personalfinancelab.com/stock-game	-Must have less than $100 in available cash, as a group, at the end of each trading day (keeps the competition balanced) -Majority vote on all transactions

TIP: Before you start Day 1, explore one of the virtual stock market sites thoroughly. Set up student and teacher accounts to you can familiarize yourself with both interfaces. The more comfortable you are with navigating options, the more fun it becomes for you and your students.

Below is general login information that may be needed for either site.

1) To register for this website, you have to use of your group member's email addresses. The site just wants to make sure a real person is registering for the site.

2) Upon choosing one person's email address, all of you will work together to create a User Name and Password that will be used to enter the site.

3) From there you must follow a series of on-screen steps to properly log in.

Make sure you write down the email address, user name, and password your group agreed upon below. All information below is case sensitive; pay attention to every letter you are writing down.

Email_____

User Name_____

Password_____

FINANCIAL
FOOTPRINT VENTURES

Understanding Your Portfolio

Beginning Monthly Portfolio Value: (Cash Available + Total Stock Value) as of the first day of the month before the market opens.

Ticker: A short series of letters representing a Company's name.

Qty: The number of shares you have for that ticker.

Current Price: This number shows the price it costs right now to buy one share of stock. It changes between 6:30am and 1:00pm (when the stock market is open).

Previous Close: The price of one share of stock as of last night's closing bell (2:00 pm)

Change: This number tells you the **change in price** for that ticker from the previous day's closing price.

Change (%): This number tells you the **percentage change** in price for that ticker from the previous day's closing price.

Purchase Price: This is the price you paid if you purchased just **one share** of the company's stock.

Gain: The total dollar gained or loss for a particular stock. It is calculated as follows (Current Value – (Purchase * Quantity))

Gain (%): The total dollar gained or loss for a particular stock. It is calculated as follows (Current Value – Total Purchase Price) * 100

Current Value: This is equal to (Current Price * Quantity)

Cash Available: This is the amount of money you have, aside from the value of your stock holdings
- Buying a stock decreases your cash
- Selling a stock raises your cash
-

Current Portfolio Value: Cash available + Current stock value

Rankings: Rankings are based on the percent return on your portfolio since the start of the month, and they are calculated at the end of each trading day. It is calculated as follows:

Percent Return = ((Current Portfolio Value – Starting Value)/Starting Value * 100

Current News (1st and 2nd Company)

Before your group decides on how much stock of a certain company to buy or sell, you should know the current news of the stock and/or the industry it is in. Following current news is vital to your group's success. It would not be advantageous to not sell shares of one of your companies that is about to be sued due to unforeseen legal matters. Additionally, you would be upset if you did not purchase extra shares of a company that is introducing a brand-new technology that is going to revolutionize its industry. You are investing, so nothing is certain, but the more educated you are in **your** stock, the more confident you will be when speaking to your group.

Date_____Day #_____ Industry_____

1st Company_____Ticker_____

SCAN ME

Current News (Indicate the website you retrieved it from)

_____

_____

_____

_____

Is this News/Dirt positive or negative to your company?_____

Based upon what you uncovered above, will you want to see or buy additional shares of your corporation_____?

Explain why_____

Date_____Day #_____ Industry_____

2nd Company_____Ticker_____

Current News (Indicate the website you retrieved it from)

_____

_____

_____

_____

Is this News/Dirt positive or negative to your company?_____

Based upon what you uncovered above, will you want to see or buy additional shares of your corporation_____?

Explain why_____

FINANCIAL
FOOTPRINT VENTURES

Day to Day Progress of Stocks (1ˢᵗ and 2ⁿᵈ Company)

Before you or your group makes any adjustments to your portfolio, fill in all lines below with information from your two companies. This will help you gain insight as to how your individual companies are performing before you make stock transactions. ***All of this information can be found on the Virtual Stock Market Game.***

Date_____ Day #_____

1st Company Name_____ Industry_____

Ticker Symbol_____

Quantity (How many shares you have in this company)_____

Price Paid_____ Last Price_____

Market Value (Current Value of stock invested in the company)_____

Total profit/loss _____

% Return (Total percent gain/loss of a particular stock)_____

Group Ranking_____

Date_____ Day #_____

2ⁿᵈ Company Name_____ Industry_____

Ticker Symbol_____

Quantity (How many shares you have in this company)_____

Price Paid_____ Last Price_____

Market Value (Current Value of stock invested in the company)_____

Total profit/loss _____

% Return (Total percent gain/loss of a particular stock)_____

Group Ranking_____

FINANCIAL
FOOTPRINT VENTURES

My Example of Utilizing Standard Deviation

L_1

*My Company Name*_____ *Day* _____
*My Company Ticker*_____ *Date* _____

Standard Deviation (S.ID.2/3) – Using monthly stock prices from the last 12 months
1-Var Stats

n (Population size) =

$\sum$x (Sum of population size) =

$\bar{x}$ /μ (Mean/Average) =

σ (Sigma: Standard Deviation) =

Based upon the data above, what does the standard deviation say about this particular stock's pattern of value at the 68%, 95% and 99% measure?

Looking at your "sigma" and your 99% measure, what is your view of this company's volatility (riskiness)?_____ Also, how will the volatility affect your decision to buy or sell shares of this company_____

FINANCIAL
FOOTPRINT VENTURES

L₁	1st Industry Company Name_____ Day_____ Company Ticker_____ Date _____ Standard Deviation (S.ID.2/3) - **Use monthly stock prices from the last 12 months** 1-Var Stats n (Population size) = $\sum$x (Sum of population size) = $\bar{x}$ /μ (Mean/Average) = σ (Sigma: Standard Deviation) =
	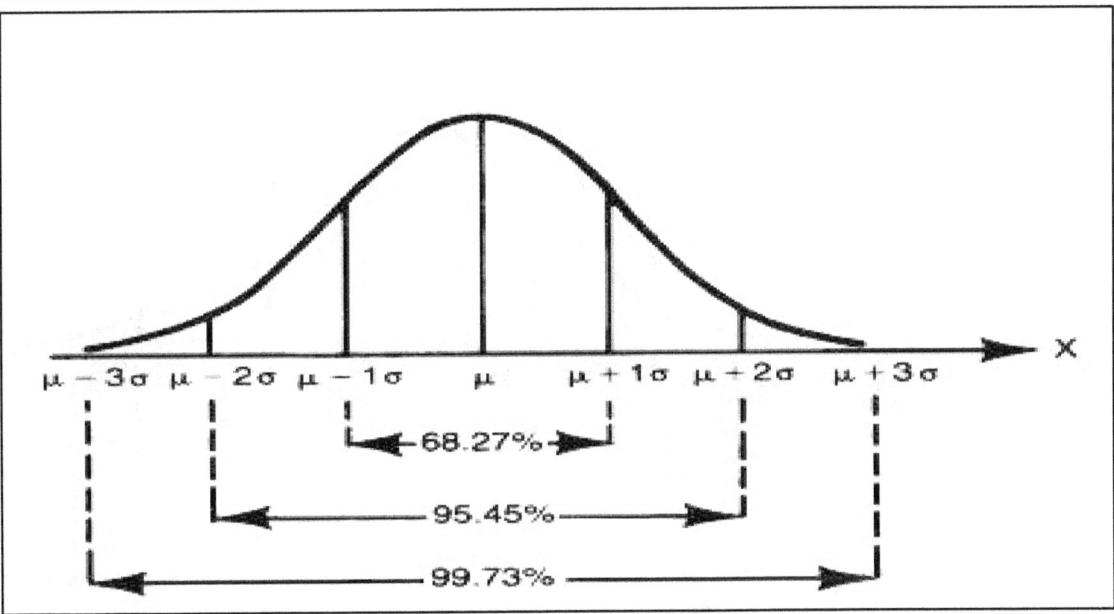

Based upon the data above, what does the standard deviation say about this particular stock's pattern of value at the 68%, 95% and 99% measure?

Looking at your "sigma" and your 99% measure, what is your view of this company's volatility (riskiness)?_____ Also, how will the volatility affect your decision to buy or sell shares of this company_____

L_1	
	2nd Industry Company Name_____ **Day**_____ **Company Ticker**_____ **Date** _____
	<u>Standard Deviation (S.ID.2/3)</u> - **Use monthly stock prices from the last 12 months** <u>1-Var Stats</u>
	n (Population size) =
	Σx (Sum of population size) =
	X̄ /μ (Mean/Average) =
	σ (Sigma: Standard Deviation) =

Based upon the data above, what does the standard deviation say about this particular stock's pattern of value at the 68%, 95% and 99% measure?

Looking at your "sigma" and your 99% measure, what is your view of this company's volatility (riskiness)?_____ Also, how will the volatility affect your decision to buy or sell shares of this company_____

FINANCIAL
FOOTPRINT VENTURES

Current News (1st and 2nd Company)

SCAN ME

Date_____Day #_____ Industry_____
1st Company_____Ticker_____
Current News (Indicate the website you retrieved it from)

_____

_____

_____

_____

Is this News/Dirt positive or negative to your company?_____
Based upon what you uncovered above, will you want to see or buy additional
shares of your corporation_____?
Explain why_____

Date_____Day #_____ Industry_____
2nd Company_____Ticker_____
Current News (Indicate the website you retrieved it from)

_____

_____

_____

_____

Is this News/Dirt positive or negative to your company?_____
Based upon what you uncovered above, will you want to see or buy additional
shares of your corporation_____?
Explain why_____

Day to Day Progress of Stocks (1st and 2nd Company)

On this document you will track the day-to-day progress of your individual companies. Fill in all lines below each time you are adjusting your portfolio.

Date_____ Day #_____

1st Company _____ Industry_____

Ticker Symbol_____

Quantity (How many shares you have in this company)_____

Price Paid_____ Last Price_____

Market Value (Current Value of stock invested in the company)_____

Total profit/loss _____

% Return (Total percent gain/loss of a particular stock)_____

Group Ranking_____

Date_____ Day #_____

2nd Company _____ Industry_____

Ticker Symbol_____

Quantity (How many shares you have in this company)_____

Price Paid_____ Last Price_____

Market Value (Current Value of stock invested in the company)_____

Total profit/loss _____

% Return (Total percent gain/loss of a particular stock)_____

Group Ranking_____

FINANCIAL
FOOTPRINT VENTURES

L₁	
	1st Industry Company Name_____ **Day**_____ **Company Ticker**_____ **Date**_____ Standard Deviation (S.ID.2/3) – **Use weekly stock prices from the past 12 weeks** 1-Var Stats n (Population size) = ∑x (Sum of population size) = x̄ /μ (Mean/Average) = σ (Sigma: Standard Deviation) =

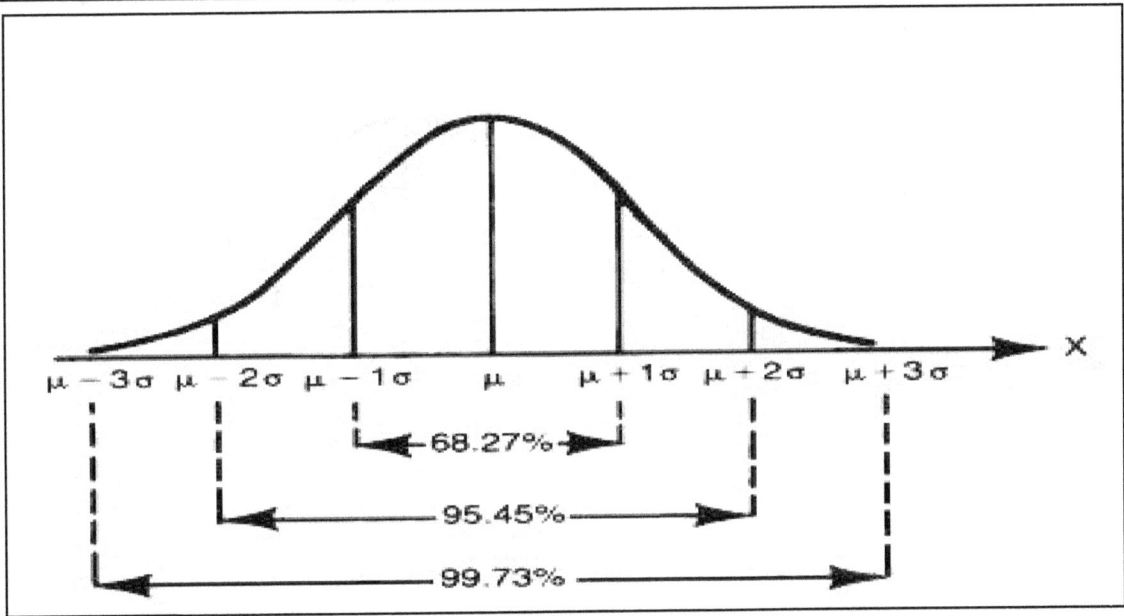

Based upon the data above, what does the standard deviation say about this particular stock's pattern of value at the 68%, 95% and 99% measure?

Looking at your "sigma" and your 99% measure, what is your view of this company's volatility (riskiness)?_____ Also, how will the volatility affect your decision to buy or sell shares of this company_____

FINANCIAL
FOOTPRINT VENTURES

L₁

*2nd Industry Company Name*_____ *Day*_____
*Company Ticker*_____ *Date*_____

Standard Deviation (S.ID.2/3) – **Use weekly stock prices from the past 12 weeks**
1-Var Stats

n (Population size) =

Σx (Sum of population size) =

$\overline{X}$ /μ (Mean/Average) =

σ (Sigma: Standard Deviation) =

Based upon the data above, what does the standard deviation say about this particular stock's pattern of value at the 68%, 95% and 99% measure?

Looking at your "sigma" and your 99% measure, what is your view of this company's volatility (riskiness)?_____ Also, how will the volatility affect your decision to buy or sell shares of this company_____

FINANCIAL
FOOTPRINT VENTURES

Current News (1st and 2nd Company)

SCAN ME

Date_____ Industry_____
1st Company_____Ticker_____
Current News (Indicate the website you retrieved it from)

_____

_____

_____

_____

Is this News/Dirt positive or negative to your company?_____
Based upon what you uncovered above, will you want to see or buy additional
shares of your corporation_____?
Explain why_____

Date_____ Industry_____
2nd Company_____Ticker_____
Current News (Indicate the website you retrieved it from)

_____

_____

_____

_____

Is this News/Dirt positive or negative to your company?_____
Based upon what you uncovered above, will you want to see or buy additional
shares of your corporation_____?
Explain why_____

Day to Day Progress of Stocks (1ˢᵗ and 2ⁿᵈ Company)

On this document you will track the day-to-day progress of your individual companies. Fill in all lines below each time you are adjusting your portfolio.

Date_____ Day #_____

1st Company _____ Industry_____

Ticker Symbol_____

Quantity (How many shares you have in this company)_____

Price Paid_____ Last Price_____

Market Value (Current Value of stock invested in the company)_____

Total profit/loss _____

% Return (Total percent gain/loss of a particular stock)_____

Group Rankings_____

Date_____ Day #_____

2ⁿᵈ Company _____ Industry_____

Ticker Symbol_____

Quantity (How many shares you have in this company)_____

Price Paid_____ Last Price_____

Market Value (Current Value of stock invested in the company)_____

Total profit/loss _____

% Return (Total percent gain/loss of a particular stock)_____

Group Rankings_____

FINANCIAL
FOOTPRINT VENTURES

L_1	
	1st Industry Company Name_____ **Day**_____
	Company Ticker_____ **Date** _____
	Standard Deviation (S.ID.2/3) – **Use daily stock prices from the past 12 days**
	1-Var Stats
	n (Population size) =
	$\sum$x (Sum of population size) =
	$\bar{x}$ /μ (Mean/Average) =
	σ (Sigma: Standard Deviation) =

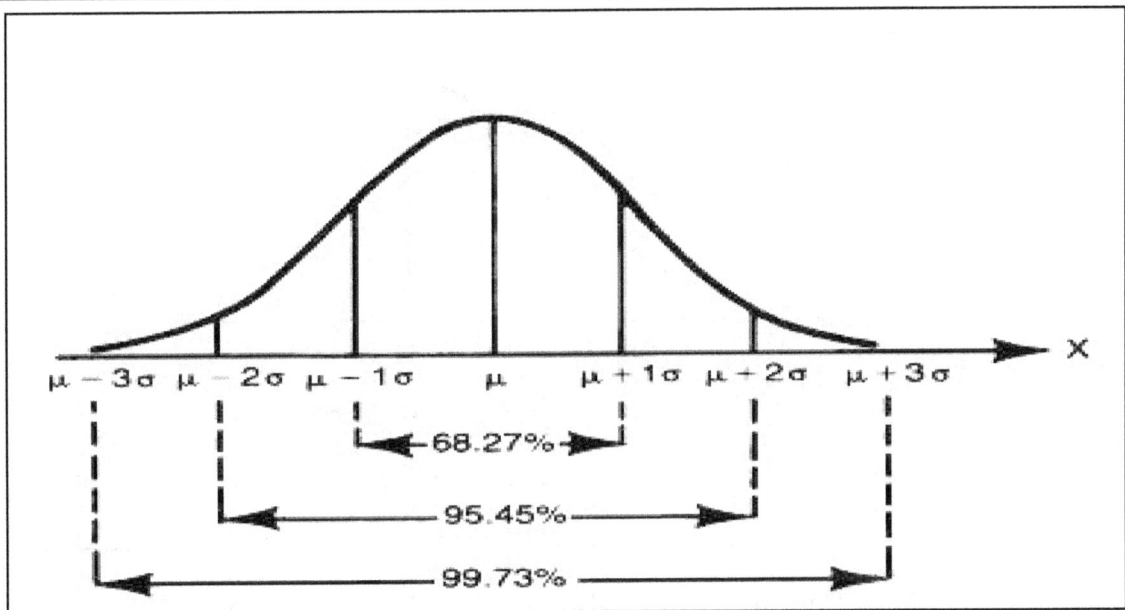

Based upon the data above, what does the standard deviation say about this particular stock's pattern of value at the 68%, 95% and 99% measure?

Looking at your "sigma" and your 99% measure, what is your view of this company's volatility (riskiness)?_____ Also, how will the volatility affect your decision to buy or sell shares of this company_____

L_1

2nd Industry Company Name_____ **Day** _____
Company Ticker_____ **Date** _____

Standard Deviation (S.ID.2/3) – **Use daily stock prices from the past 12 days**
1-Var Stats

n (Population size) =

$\sum$x (Sum of population size) =

$\bar{x}$ /μ (Mean/Average) =

σ (Sigma: Standard Deviation) =

Based upon the data above, what does the standard deviation say about this particular stock's pattern of value at the 68%, 95% and 99% measure?

Looking at your "sigma" and your 99% measure, what is your view of this company's volatility (riskiness)?_____ Also, how will the volatility affect your decision to buy or sell shares of this company_____

FINANCIAL
FOOTPRINT VENTURES

Current News (1st and 2nd Company)

SCAN ME

Date_____Day #_____ Industry_____
1st Company_____Ticker_____
Current News (Indicate the website you retrieved it from)

_____

_____

_____

_____

Is this News/Dirt positive or negative to your company?_____
Based upon what you uncovered above, will you want to see or buy additional
shares of your corporation_____?
Explain why_____

Date_____Day #_____ Industry_____
2nd Company_____Ticker_____
Current News (Indicate the website you retrieved it from)

_____

_____

_____

_____

Is this News/Dirt positive or negative to your company?_____
Based upon what you uncovered above, will you want to see or buy additional
shares of your corporation_____?
Explain why_____

Day to Day Progress of Stocks (1st and 2nd Company)

On this document you will track the day-to-day progress of your individual companies. Fill in all lines below each time you are adjusting your portfolio.

Date_____ Day #_____

1st Company _____ Industry_____

Ticker Symbol_____

Quantity (How many shares you have in this company)_____

Price Paid_____ Last Price_____

Market Value (Current Value of stock invested in the company)_____

Total profit/loss _____

% Return (Total percent gain/loss of a particular stock)_____

Group Rankings_____

Date_____ Day #_____

2nd Company _____ Industry_____

Ticker Symbol_____

Quantity (How many shares you have in this company)_____

Price Paid_____ Last Price_____

Market Value (Current Value of stock invested in the company)_____

Total profit/loss _____

% Return (Total percent gain/loss of a particular stock)_____

Group Rankings_____

FINANCIAL
FOOTPRINT VENTURES

L₁

1ˢᵗ Industry Company Name_____ **Day**_____

Company Ticker_____ **Date** _____

Standard Deviation (S.ID.2/3) – **Use daily stock prices from the past 12 days**
1-Var Stats

n (Population size) =

∑x (Sum of population size) =

x̄ /μ (Mean/Average) =

σ (Sigma: Standard Deviation) =

$\mu - 3\sigma$ $\mu - 2\sigma$ $\mu - 1\sigma$ μ $\mu + 1\sigma$ $\mu + 2\sigma$ $\mu + 3\sigma$

68.27%
95.45%
99.73%

Based upon the data above, what does the standard deviation say about this particular stock's pattern of value at the 68%, 95% and 99% measure?

Looking at your "sigma" and your 99% measure, what is your view of this company's volatility (riskiness)?_____ Also, how will the volatility affect your decision to buy or sell shares of this company_____

L₁

2nd Industry Company Name_____ **Day** _____

Company Ticker_____ **Date** _____

Standard Deviation (S.ID.2/3) – **Use daily stock prices from the past 12 days**
1-Var Stats

n (Population size) =

∑x (Sum of population size) =

x̄ /μ (Mean/Average) =

σ (Sigma: Standard Deviation) =

Based upon the data above, what does the standard deviation say about this particular stock's pattern of value at the 68%, 95% and 99% measure?

Looking at your "sigma" and your 99% measure, what is your view of this company's volatility (riskiness)?_____ Also, how will the volatility affect your decision to buy or sell shares of this company_____

FINANCIAL
FOOTPRINT VENTURES

Total Amount Gained (Entire portfolio)

For this competition you and your group mates have become **equity investors**. This means you have invested a large sum of money (in your case $1 million) in the hopes of using the profits from these companies for a larger purchase (hypothetically) or to win the competition (literally).

The information below can be found on the "Rankings" Page. Select "Overall".

Current Portfolio Value (C.P.V) - Your overall portfolio at the top of the dashboard.
Initial Portfolio Value (I.P.V) – This value is the $1,000,000 you started with.
Total Amount Gained (T.A.G/L) – Amount your stocks have gained or lost.

Date_____   Date_____
Day #_____   Day #_____

C.P.V_____   C.P.V_____
- I.P.V_____   - I.P.V_____
= T.A.G_____   = T.A.G_____

Date_____   Date_____
Day #_____   Day #_____

C.P.V_____   C.P.V_____
- I.P.V_____   - I.P.V_____
= T.A.G_____   = T.A.G_____

Date_____   Date_____
Day #_____   Day #_____

C.P.V_____   C.P.V_____
- I.P.V_____   - I.P.V_____
= T.A.G_____   = T.A.G_____

FINANCIAL
FOOTPRINT VENTURES

Non-Investing Standard Deviation Practice

1). Mike asked 200 people to run for 13 seconds. He recorded each distance for all 200 people. He found the distances were normally distributed with a mean of 72 meters and a standard deviation of 8 meters.

Complete the Normal Standard Bell Curve below using the information above.

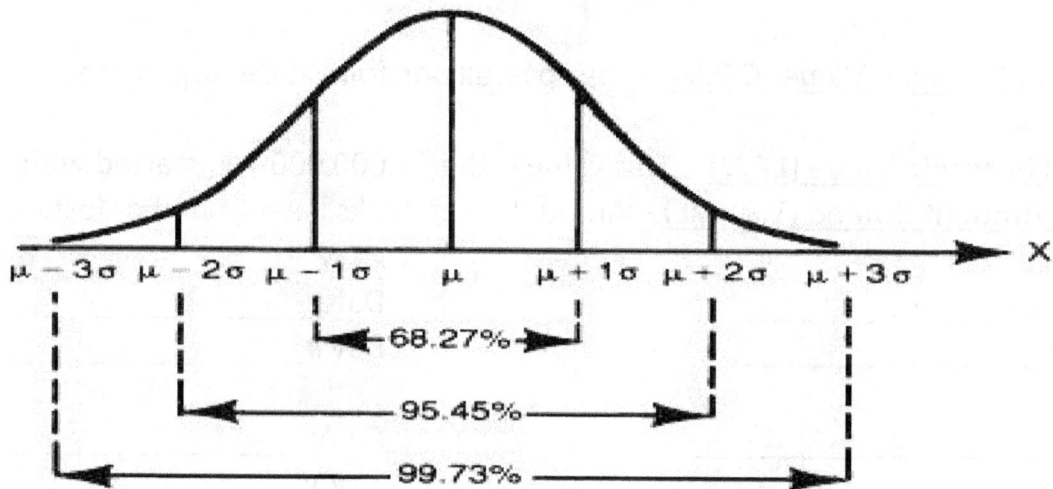

For each scenario below, select whether Value A is greater, Value B is greater, or the values are equal. Place an "X" to signify your response.

	Value A is Greater	Value B is Greater	Equal
Value A: The mean distance of runners within ±1 standard dev of the mean. **Value B:** The mean distance of all the runners.			
Show work to justify your selection above:			
Value A: The number of people who ran between 88 and 96 meters. **Value B:** The number of people who ran between 48 and 64 meters.			
Show work to justify your selection above:			
Value A: The number of people who ran ±2 standard dev of the mean. **Value B:** The number of people who ran ±1 standard dev of the mean.			
Show work to justify your selection above:			

FINANCIAL
FOOTPRINT VENTURES

2). The app store sells apps that range in price from $6.85 to $13.50. A new app that costs $2.35 is added to the selection. You choose to substitute one of your older – outlier apps for the new one. Select whether the value of each statistic for the range of app prices increases, decreases, or is not affected when the new app price is added. *Use the blank space below to illustrate your thinking as best as possible.*

	Increases	Decreases	Is not affected
Mean			
Provide an explanation for your selection above:			
Median			
Provide an explanation for your selection above:			
Standard Deviation			
Provide an explanation for your selection above:			

3). You work for an organization that is totally funded by lawsuits based on faulty airline mile redemptions. A certain airline claims the miles provided in 14 different policies are normally distributed, with a mean of 50,000 miles and a standard deviation of 20,000 miles. You analyze the 14 policies and record the findings below.

78,421	71,890	58,276	52,104	45,743	65,392	61,910
37,124	32,760	27,890	16,874	76,473	63,100	48,372

i). Find the mean and median of the findings above use the symbols to indicate
mean: standard deviation:
median:

ii). Complete the Standard Normal Bell Curve below with the information from question "i" above.

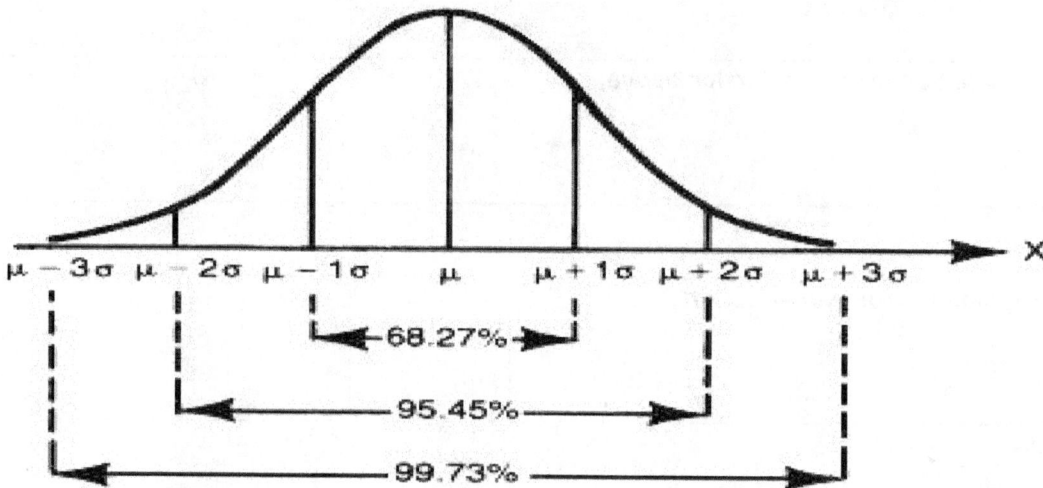

iii). Compare the mean and standard deviation of your sample with those in the airline miles redemption claim. Provide a detailed explanation as to what you noticed.

FINANCIAL
FOOTPRINT VENTURES

4). Sketch the following normal curves:

(a) with mean 17 and standard deviation 3
(b) with mean 16 and standard deviation 3
(c) with mean 17 and standard deviation 4
(d) with mean 16 and standard deviation 4
(e) Consider two normal curves from the scenarios above. If one has a larger mean, must it have a larger standard deviation as well? Provide reasons as to your response below.

5) What percentage of the area under the normal curve lies
(a) Between $\mu - 2\sigma$ and $\mu + 2\sigma$

(b) Between $\mu - 3\sigma$ and $\mu + 3\sigma$

(c) Between $\mu - \sigma$ and $\mu + \sigma$

6) Trees can be researched when figuring out the prehistoric dates of people. Tree-ring dating is the process archaeologists use to discover these prehistoric dates. Tree humps from several excavation sites were evenly distributed, had mound shaped distributions and were symmetric about the mean. They had a μ of 1456 (years) and a σ of 42 (years). Use the Empirical Rule to do the following:

(a) Estimate a range of years centered about the mean in which about 68% of the data will be found.

(b) Estimate a range of years centered about the mean in which about 95% of the data will be found.

(c) Estimate a range of years centered about the mean in which almost all of the data will be found.

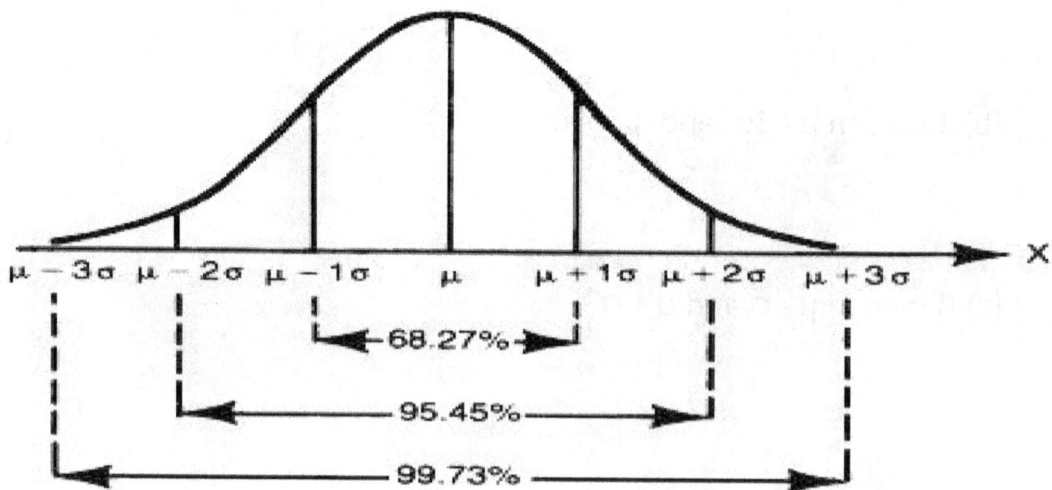

FINANCIAL
FOOTPRINT VENTURES

Name_____Date_____Period_____

Standard Deviation Formative Exam (Stock data must be provided)

(1pt)

L_1

*Company Name*_____
*Company Ticker*_____

Standard Deviation (S.ID.2/3)   **(4pts)**
1-Var Stats
n (Population size) =

$\sum$x (Sum of population size) =

$\bar{x}$ /μ (Mean/Average) =

σ (Sigma: Standard Deviation) =

2pts

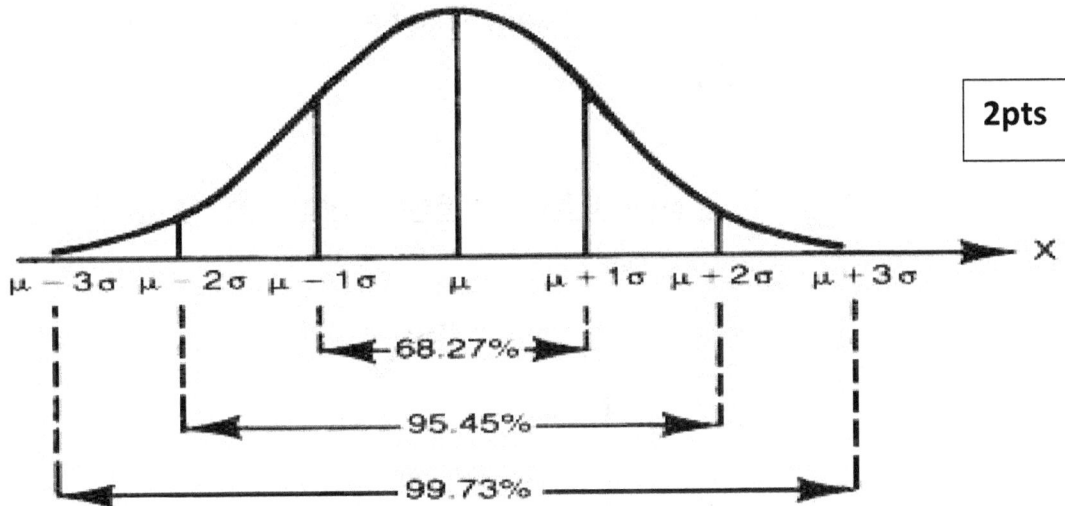

Looking at your "sigma", the 99% measure, and the historical data provided, what is your view on the volatility (riskiness) of this company and its ability to make a profit? You must include the following terms in your answer: *sigma, 99% measure, market cap, historical data.* **(2pts)**

The gas bill is a vital expense when you have a place of your own. The following is a list of my monthly gas bills for the last 11 months.

$133 $112 $128 $147 $87 $68 $94 $156 $90 $87 $139

Cut your answers off at the hundredths place.

A) What is the monthly mean gas bill? **(1pt)**

B) What is the median gas bill? **(1pt)**

C) What is the standard Deviation? **(1pt)**

D) What monthly bill prices above fall between the $\mu + 1\sigma$ and $\mu + 2\sigma$ measure? **(1pt)**

Complete the Standard Normal Bell Curve with the data above. **(2pts)**

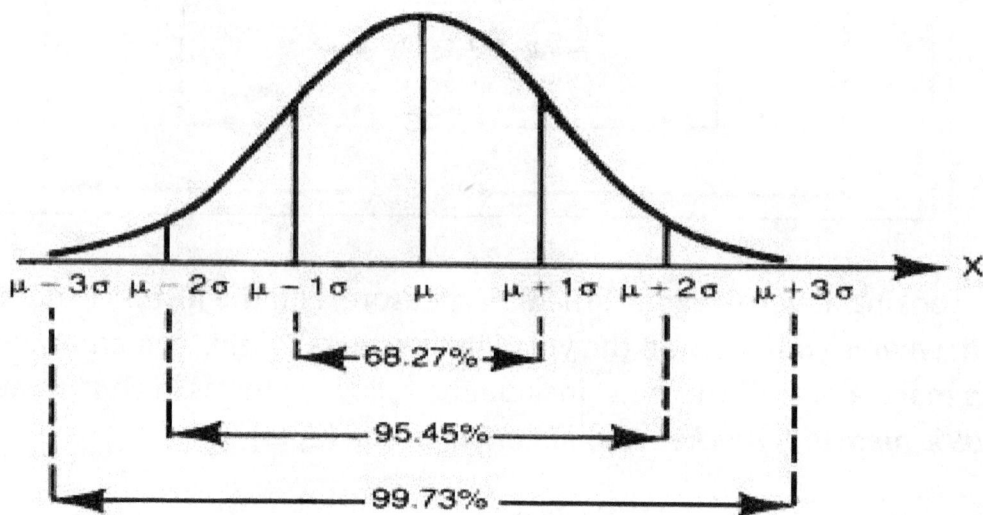

FINANCIAL
FOOTPRINT VENTURES

Scoring Breakdown

+14 to +15 = 4.0

+13 = 3.5

+12 = 3.0

+11 = 2.5

+9 to +10 = 2.0

+8 and below = 1.0

Points Correct _____

Grade_____

Common Core State Standards

CCSS.MATH.CONTENT.HSS.ID.A.1

Represent data with plots on the real number line (dot plots, histograms, and box plots).

CCSS.MATH.CONTENT.HSS.ID.A.2

Use statistics appropriate to the shape of the data distribution to compare center (median, mean) and spread (interquartile range, standard deviation) of two or more different data sets.

CCSS.MATH.CONTENT.HSS.ID.A.3

Interpret differences in shape, center, and spread in the context of the data sets, accounting for possible effects of extreme data points (outliers).

CCSS.MATH.CONTENT.HSS.ID.A.4

Use the mean and standard deviation of a data set to fit it to a normal distribution.

National Standards in K-12 Personal Finance Education

Investing

Standard 1: Investment Risk

Evaluate the relationship between risk and return.

Standard 2: Investment Strategies

Differentiate between diversified and non-diversified portfolios.

Standard 3: Investment Planning

Explain the purposes of various investment options.

Council for Economic Education (CEE): National Standards for Financial Decision Making

Financial Decision Making

Standard 1. Recognize the responsibilities associated with personal financial decisions.

Standard 4. Make criterion-based financial decisions by systematically considering alternatives and consequences

Saving and Investing

Standard 2. Use reliable resources when making financial decisions.

FINANCIAL
FOOTPRINT VENTURES

Standards for Mathematical Practice

SMP 1: Make sense of problems and persevere in solving them

Students must interpret unfamiliar financial data (e.g., daily closing prices), define volatility in context, and persist through multi-step calculations.
They must also frame a meaningful question: Which stock is riskier? Which offers better return for the risk?

SMP 2: Reason abstractly and quantitatively

Students interpret standard deviation as a measure of spread — not just a formula, but what it means in terms of risk.
They must connect numeric volatility to investor decision-making and personal risk tolerance.

SMP 3: Construct viable arguments and critique the reasoning of others

Students present their findings and justify: Why is Stock A, a smarter investment than Stock B?
Peer-to-peer discussion fosters critique of assumptions (e.g., ignoring outliers, sample size, or market context).

SMP 4: Model with mathematics

Students model stock volatility using standard deviation, mean return, and possibly regression or trend lines.
They simulate investment scenarios and compare outcomes to model decisions over time.

SMP 5: Use appropriate tools strategically

Students use graphing calculators, Desmos/Geogebra, or finance websites (Yahoo Finance, Google Sheets) to collect, compute, and visualize.
Strategic tool use supports calculation, analysis, and presentation.

SMP 6: Attend to precision

Precision in computation is essential for accurate standard deviation values. Also includes correct terminology (e.g., "volatility," "spread," "mean," "sigma") and clear communication of findings.

SMP 7: Look for and make use of structure

Students notice patterns in volatility across industries (e.g., tech stocks = high SD; utilities = low SD).
They may recognize a stock's standard deviation as part of a larger structure — portfolio theory or historical trends.

SMP 8: Look for and express regularity in repeated reasoning

Students repeatedly calculate mean and standard deviation across different stocks or timeframes.
They may generalize conclusions (e.g., "higher return usually comes with higher risk") and begin to form investment heuristics.

FINANCIAL
FOOTPRINT VENTURES

Websites for Investing
Checking Accounts are needed for all websites below

Portfolio Building
Fundrise.com: A platform that helps you build a portfolio of private assets like real estate, private credit, and venture capital.

Stocks/Bonds/Mutual Funds/ETF's
robinhood.com: A website to purchase stocks. As little as $10 a month to get started.

Worthybonds.com: A platform that uses bond funds to lend money to individual and corporate developers of local real estate projects (including affordable housing). Worthy then pays interest on the bonds with the interest from the loans. Low entry price of $10 per bond.

ally.com: Loans, Savings Accounts, Certificates of Deposits, Investing. Self-directed trading, $4.95 per stock trade. **(Savings Accounts Also!)**

Peer to Peer Lending (How banks are extremely profitable)
solofunds.com: A website where you can lend money to individuals and they pay you back with interest. No minimum, lend what you want when you want.

Real Estate
Collabhome.io: Invest in student housing to earn monthly income. Start with $100.

Angel Investing (The act of providing funds to early-stage startup companies)
startengine.com: You are able to invest in the very early stages of corporation. Angel investing can be extremely profitable if the company goes public or is bought out.

microventures.com: Private market investment opportunities (early-stage investment into corporations)

Scope and Sequence/Unit Calendar

Some activities may take more time than what is allotted on this calendar. Additionally, you may take out activities you feel add more time than you can a lot. This is not a rigid calendar. Adjust the activities to your students' needs.

Day/Date	Class Work	Investment Practice/HW
Day 1 **Date**_____	Pass out $5 investment pitch **Pgs. 9 – 10** -Start "Interest" activities **Pgs. 11 – 15**	-$5 investment due by the Day 10. -Complete "Interest" activities **Pgs. 11 - 15**
Day 2 **Date**_____	**Class Work** Review "Interest" activities **Pgs. 11 - 15** -Start 10 tips for Picking Stock Winners **Pg. 19** - Reading Stock Data/Additional Vocabulary to find **Pgs. 20 - 21**	**Investment Practice/HW** -Complete 10 Tips for Picking Stock Winners **Pg. 19** -Reading Stock Data **Pgs. 20 - 21**

FINANCIAL
FOOTPRINT VENTURES

	Class Work	Investment Practice/HW
Day 3 **Date**_____	Review 10 Tips for Picking Stock Winners **Pg. 19** Review Reading Stock Data/Additional Vocabulary to find **Pgs. 20 – 21** -Start Contextual Example (Industries and Companies) **Pgs. 22 – 23**	-\$5 investment due by the Day 10. -Start Selection of 2 Industries/Companies + Market Cap **Pgs. 24 - 25**
Day 4 **Date**_____	**Class Work** -Continue Selection of 2 Industries/Companies + Market Cap **Pgs. 24 - 25**	Investment Practice/HW -\$5 investment due by the Day 10. - Finish Selection of 2 Industries/Companies + Market Cap **Pgs. 24 – 25**

	Class Work	Investment Practice/HW
Day 5 **Date**_____	-Finish Selection of 2 Industries/Companies + Market Cap **Pgs. 24 - 25**	-$5 investment due by the Day 10. - Finish Selection of 2 Industries/Companies + Market Cap **Pgs. 24 – 25**
Day 6 **Date**_____	-Start Price to Earnings Ratio Analyzing 2 companies in 1st Industry **Pgs. 26 - 27** -Start Price to Book Ratio Analyzing 2 companies in 1st Industry **Pgs. 28 - 29**	-$5 investment due by the Day 10. -Continue Price to Earnings Ratio Analyzing 2 companies in 1st Industry **Pgs. 26 - 27** -**Continue** Price to Book Ratio Analyzing 2 companies in 1st Industry **Pgs. 28 – 29**

FINANCIAL
FOOTPRINT VENTURES

Day 7 Date_____	**Class Work** -Continue/Finish Price to Earnings Ratio Analyzing 2 companies in 1st Industry **Pgs. 26 - 27** -Continue/Finish Price to Book Ratio Analyzing 2 companies in 1st Industry **Pgs. 28 - 29**	**Investment Practice/HW** -$5 investment due by the Day 10. -Finish Price to Earnings Ratio Analyzing 2 companies in 1st Industry **Pgs. 26 - 27** -Finish Price to Book Ratio Analyzing 2 companies in 1st Industry **Pgs. 28 - 29**
Day 8 Date_____	**Class Work** -Start Current Ratio Analyzing 2 companies in 1st Industry **Pgs. 30 - 31** -Start Debt to Equity Ratio Analyzing 2 companies in 1st Industry **Pgs. 32 - 33**	**Investment Practice/HW** -$5 investment due by the Day 10. -Continue Current Ratio Analyzing 2 companies in 1st Industry **Pgs. 30 - 31** -Continue Debt to Equity Ratio Analyzing 2 companies in 1st Industry **Pgs. 32 - 33**

	Class Work	Investment Practice/HW
Day 9 **Date_____**	-Continue/Finish Current Ratio Analyzing 2 companies in 1st Industry **Pgs. 30 - 31** -Continue/Finish Debt to Equity Ratio Analyzing 2 companies in 1st Industry **Pgs. 32 - 33**	-$5 investment due by tomorrow. -Finish Current Ratio Analyzing 2 companies in 1st Industry **Pgs. 30 - 31** -Finish Debt to Equity Ratio Analyzing 2 companies in 1st Industry **Pgs. 32 - 33**
Day 10 **Date_____**	-$5 investment due today. -Complete 1st company in 1st industry based upon all 4 ratios **Pg. 34** -Add 1st company in 1st industry to list of final stock selections (Also add your group members selections) **Pgs. 46 - 47**	-Start Price to Earnings Ratio Analyzing 2 companies in 2nd Industry **Pg. 35** -Start Price to Book Ratio Analyzing 2 companies in 2nd Industry **Pg. 36**

FINANCIAL
FOOTPRINT VENTURES

	Class Work	Investment Practice/HW
Day 11 **Date_____**	-Finish Price to Earnings Ratio Analyzing 2 companies in 2nd Industry **Pg. 35** -Finish Price to Book Ratio Analyzing 2 companies in 2nd Industry **Pg. 36**	-Start Current Ratio Analyzing 2 companies in 2nd Industry **Pg. 37** -Start Debt to Equity Ratio Analyzing 2 companies in 2nd Industry **Pg. 38**
Day 12 **Date_____**	-Finish Current Ratio Analyzing 2 companies in 2nd Industry **Pg. 37** -Finish Debt to Equity Ratio Analyzing 2 companies in 2nd Industry **Pg. 38** -Complete 1st company in 2nd industry based upon all 4 ratios **Pg. 39** -Add 1st company in 2nd industry to list of final stock selections (Also add your group members selections) **Pgs. 46 - 47**	-Complete 1st company in 2nd industry based upon all 4 ratios **Pg. 39** -Add 1st company in 2nd industry to list of final stock selections **Pgs. 46 - 47**

	Class Work	Investment Practice/HW
Day 13 **Date_____**	**Class Work** -Start Mean and Median Stock Price **Pgs. 40 - 42**	Investment Practice/HW -Continue Mean and Median Stock Price **Pgs. 40 - 42**
Day 14 **Date_____**	**Class Work** -Complete Mean and Median Stock Price **Pgs. 40 - 42**	Investment Practice/HW -Start Standard Deviation **Pgs. 43 - 45**
Day 15 **Date_____**	**Class Work** -Continue Standard Deviation **Pgs. 43 - 45**	Investment Practice/HW -Continue Standard Deviation **Pgs. 43 - 45**
Day 16 **Date_____**	**Class Work** -Finish Standard Deviation **Pgs. 43 - 45**	Investment Practice/HW -Finish Standard Deviation **Pgs. 43 - 45**

FINANCIAL
FOOTPRINT VENTURES

	Class Work	Investment Practice/HW
Day 17 **Date_____**	-Log into Virtual Stock Market Game (use companies from Pgs. 46 – 47) -$1,000,000 Per group -Minium $100 invested in each company (cannot be less than $100) -Must have less then $100 in available cash, as a group, at the end of each trading day (keeps the competition balanced) -Majority vote on all transactions **Pg. 48 - 49**	
Day 18 **Date_____**	**Class Work** **Continue** -Log into Virtual Stock Market Game (use companies from Pgs. 46 – 47) -$1,000,000 Per group -Minium $100 invested in each company (cannot be less than $100)) -Must have less then $100 in available cash, as a group, at the end of each trading day (keeps the competition balanced) -Majority vote on all transactions **Pg. 48 – 49**	Investment Practice/HW

FINANCIAL
FOOTPRINT VENTURES

	Class Work	Investment Practice/HW
Day 19 **Date_____**	**Continue** -Log into Virtual Stock Market Game (use companies from Pgs. 46 – 47) -$1,000,000 Per group -Minium $100 invested in each company (cannot be less than $100) -Must have less than $100 in available cash, as a group, at the end of each trading day (keeps the competition balanced) -Majority vote on all transactions **Pg. 48 – 49**	
Day 20 **Date_____**	**Class Work** -Current News on 1st and 2nd Company **Pg. 50**	Investment Practice/HW -Continue Current News on 1st and 2nd Company Pg. 50
Day 21 **Date_____**	**Class Work** -Review Current News on 1st and 2nd Company. Talk about the individual and group impact of the current news. **Pg. 50**	Investment Practice/HW -Start Day to Day Progress of Stocks (1st and 2nd Company) Pg. 51

FINANCIAL
FOOTPRINT VENTURES

	Class Work	Investment Practice/HW
Day 22 **Date**_____	-Finish Day to Day Progress of Stocks (1st and 2nd Company) - Talk about the individual and group impact of the individual stocks. **Pg. 51** -Total Amount Gained (Entire Portfolio) -How is your group measuring up? **Pg. 67**	-Review Standard Deviation Pgs. 43 - 45
Day 23 **Date**_____	-My Example of Utilizing Standard Deviation **Pg. 52**	-Start Standard Deviation of last 12 months stock price (company 1 and 2) **Pgs. 53 - 54**
Day 24 **Date**_____	- Continue Standard Deviation of last 12 months stock price (company 1 and 2) **Pgs. 53 – 54**	-Finish Standard Deviation of last 12 months stock price (company 1 and 2) **Pgs. 53 - 54**

	Class Work	Investment Practice/HW
Day 25 **Date_____**	- Review Standard Deviation of last 12 months stock price (company 1 and 2) - How do these numbers impact your decision to buy/sell stocks? **Pgs. 53 – 54**	
Day 26 **Date_____**	**Post the group rankings in the class** -Adjust your portfolios on the Virtual Stock Market Game -Minium $100 invested in each company (cannot be less than $100) -Must have less than $100 in available cash, as a group, at the end of each trading day -Majority vote on all transactions **Pgs. 46 - 48**	Investment Practice/HW

FINANCIAL
FOOTPRINT VENTURES

	Class Work	Investment Practice/HW
Day 27 **Date**_____	**Class Work** -Adjust your portfolios on the Virtual Stock Market Game -Minium $100 invested in each company (cannot be less than $100) -Must have less than $100 in available cash, as a group, at the end of each trading day -Majority vote on all transactions **Pgs. 46 - 48**	**Investment Practice/HW**
Day 27 **Date**_____	**Class Work** -Non-Investing Standard Deviation Practice #1 and #2 **Pg. 68 - 69**	**Investment Practice/HW** Continue Non-Investing Standard Deviation Practice #1 and #2 Pg. 68 - 69
Day 28 **Date**_____	**Class Work** -Continue Non-Investing Standard Deviation Practice #1 and #2 **Pg. 68 - 69**	**Investment Practice/HW** Finish Non-Investing Standard Deviation Practice #1 and #2 Pg. 68 - 69
Day 29 **Date**_____	**Class Work** -Discuss Non-Investing Standard Deviation Practice #1 and #2 **Pg. 68 - 69**	**Investment Practice/HW** -Current News on 1st and 2nd Company Pg. 55

	Class Work	Investment Practice/HW
Day 30 **Date_____**	-Review Current News on 1st and 2nd Company. Talk about the individual and group impact of the current news. **Pg. 55** -Start Day to Day Progress of Stocks (1st and 2nd Company) **Pg. 56**	-Continue Day to Day Progress of Stocks (1st and 2nd Company) **Pg. 56**
Day 31 **Date_____**	-Finish Day to Day Progress of Stocks (1st and 2nd Company) - Talk about the individual and group impact of the individual stocks. **Pg. 56** -Total Amount Gained (Entire Portfolio) -How is your group measuring up? **Pg. 67**	Investment Practice/HW

FINANCIAL
FOOTPRINT VENTURES

	Class Work	Investment Practice/HW
Day 32 **Date_____**	**Post the group rankings in the class** - Review Standard Deviation of last 12 weeks stock price (company 1 and 2) - How do these numbers impact your decision to buy/sell stocks? **Pgs. 57 – 58** -Adjust your portfolios on the Virtual Stock Market Game -Minium $100 invested in each company (cannot be less than $100) -Must have less than $100 in available cash, as a group, at the end of each trading day -Majority vote on all transactions **Pgs. 46 - 48**	- Continue Standard Deviation of last 12 weeks stock price (company 1 and 2) - How do these numbers impact your decision to buy/sell stocks? **Pgs. 57 – 58**

	Class Work	Investment Practice/HW
Day 33 **Date**_____	-Adjust your portfolios on the Virtual Stock Market Game -Minium $100 invested in each company (cannot be less than $100) -Must have less than $100 in available cash, as a group, at the end of each trading day -Majority vote on all transactions **Pgs. 46 - 48**	
Day 34 **Date**_____	**Class Work** -Non-Investing Standard Deviation Practice #3, #4 and #5 **Pg. 70 - 71**	**Investment Practice/HW** Continue Non-Investing Standard Deviation Practice #3, #4 and #5 **Pg. 70 - 71**
Day 35 **Date**_____	**Class Work** -Continue Non-Investing Standard Deviation Practice #3, #4 and #5 **Pg. 70 - 71**	**Investment Practice/HW** Finish Non-Investing Standard Deviation Practice #3, #4 and #5 **Pg. 70 - 71**

FINANCIAL
FOOTPRINT VENTURES

	Class Work	Investment Practice/HW
Day 36 Date_____	-Discuss Non-Investing Standard Deviation Practice #3, #4 and #5 **Pg. 70 - 71**	-Current News on 1st and 2nd Company **Pg. 63**
Day 37 Date_____	**Class Work** -Review Current News on 1st and 2nd Company. Talk about the individual and group impact of the current news. **Pg. 63** -Start Day to Day Progress of Stocks (1st and 2nd Company) **Pg. 64**	**Investment Practice/HW** -Continue Day to Day Progress of Stocks (1st and 2nd Company) **Pg. 64**
Day 38 Date_____	**Class Work** -Finish Day to Day Progress of Stocks (1st and 2nd Company) - Talk about the individual and group impact of the individual stocks. **Pg. 64** -Total Amount Gained (Entire Portfolio) -How is your group measuring up? **Pg. 67**	**Investment Practice/HW**

	Class Work	Investment Practice/HW
Day 39 Date_____	**Post the group rankings in the class** - Review Standard Deviation of last 12 days stock price (company 1 and 2) - How do these numbers impact your decision to buy/sell stocks? **Pgs. 65 - 66** -Adjust your portfolios on the Virtual Stock Market Game -Minium $100 invested in each company (cannot be less than $100) -Must have less than $100 in available cash, as a group, at the end of each trading day -Majority vote on all transactions **Pgs. 46 - 48**	Continue Standard Deviation of last 12 days stock price (company 1 and 2) - How do these numbers impact your decision to buy/sell stocks? **Pgs. 65 - 66**
	Class Work	**Investment Practice/HW**
Day 40 Date_____	-Non-Investing Standard Deviation Practice $6 **Pg. 72**	Continue Non-Investing Standard Deviation Practice #6 Pg. 72

FINANCIAL
FOOTPRINT VENTURES

	Class Work	Investment Practice/HW

Day 40
Date_____
	-Discuss Non-Investing Standard Deviation Practice #6
	Pg. 72
		-Review all Non-Investing Standard Deviation Practice Problems
		Pgs. 68 - 72
		
		-Review the following Standard Deviation stock analysis pages:
		• Last 12 months
		   Pgs. 53 - 54
		• Last 12 Weeks
		   Pgs. 57 - 58
		• Last 12 Days
		   Pgs. 61 – 62

Day 41
Date_____
	-Discuss all Non-Investing Standard Deviation Practice Problems
	Pgs. 68 - 72
	
	-Discuss the following Standard Deviation stock analysis pages:
	• Last 12 months
	   Pgs. 53 - 54
	• Last 12 Weeks
	   Pgs. 57 - 58
	• Last 12 Days
	   Pgs. 61 – 62
		-Review all Non-Investing Standard Deviation Practice Problems
		Pgs. 68 - 72
		
		-Review the following Standard Deviation stock analysis pages:
		• Last 12 months
		   Pgs. 53 - 54
		• Last 12 Weeks
		   Pgs. 57 - 58
		• Last 12 Days
		   Pgs. 61 – 62

	Class Work	Investment Practice/HW
Day 42 **Date**_____	-Start Non-Investing Standard Deviation Formative Exam **Pgs. 73 – 74** **(Page 75 is for grading)**	
Day 43 **Date**_____	**Class Work** -Complete Non-Investing Standard Deviation Formative Exam **Pgs. 73 – 74** **(Page 75 is for grading)**	Investment Practice/HW